Tl

Christmas

Holiday Mixology Magic

Published by La Flama Azul Press
EDITORIAL OFFICE:
La Flama Azul
6051 Business Center Ct. 4-275, San Diego, CA 92154
Editorial and production: John Seeley
Type design and typography: Bob Adams
Formatting by L.L. Holter
Cover design: Sara Matte
Cover photo by Sitara Perez, c. 2021

Library of Congress Cataloguing-in-Publication Data
Perez, Sitara Monica.
The 12 Drinks of Christmas / Sitara Monica Perez
ISBN: 978-1-945533-06-8
Printed in the USA on acid-free paper
Distributed by Blue Moon Wonders
10 9 8 7 6 5 4 3 2 1

Manufactured in the United States

First Edition

This book is dedicated to the good people who enjoy wine and spirits. May you find new ways here to enjoy and share with friends!

Acknowledgements

I want to thank my talented boyfriend and partner in crime, Todd Truelson for his vision and hard work bringing the distilling project to life. And I want to thank my friend and colleague Kate Reifers for her unwavering good energy and for being my one woman focus group. And thank you to all of our La Flama Azúl cocktail enthusiasts!!! Last but not least, a big shout out to John Seeley for inspiring, editing and publishing this book.

OUR SPIRITS

Utilizing his own custom-built column still, Todd distills local wine to create exceptional grape-based spirits. His triple distilled vodka is silky, fruity, and floral and fans rave about its surprising sippability. His unbarreled brandy, otherwise known as eau de vie, has even more fruit expression and is a favorite of Sitara's when creating craft cocktails. Their Berry Brandy is infused with a medley of berries and hibiscus. It is delightfully smooth, fragrant, and lightly sweetened. Most fans are happy to sip it neat, but it is also absolutely gorgeous in craft cocktails. The mildly spicy/sweet Cinnamon Schnapps is a sexy sipper, lovely on its own or in mixed drinks. And last but not least their flagship spirit, the F150 Fennel Liqueur is a highly distinctive expression of their sunny Baja California home. To flavor this unique distillate, Todd and Sitara hand-forage the ripe seeds of wild fennel that grows by the roadsides. Though compared to anise flavored spirits and licorice, the F150 is in a class all its own. Fans sip it neat, occasionally with a cube of ice, while Sitara adores slipping in small amounts when building her cocktail recipes for that *je ne sais quoi.*

Currently Todd and Sitara are developing their new gin project, an apricot brandy as well as a barrel-aged brandy. They plan to tackle whiskeys too. Stay tuned.

La Flama Azúl, our distillery and private membership cocktail club

Table of Contents

Introduction

This recipe book is inspired by the holidays. Each drink is a festive tribute to friends and family. It's about celebration and connection. I hope that you find these tasty concoctions satiate your palate and all of your senses. May you share many fun memories and enjoy these luscious libations for many years to come. Begin new traditions and create moments that you will treasure forever!

The Christmas holiday season is a time like no other. As much a test of food and drink endurance as it is a time of celebration with friends and family. And Christmas is the one day of the year when folks who wouldn't dream of drinking alcohol with breakfast, not only start their day with something stronger than their usual coffee, but then go to drink through morning, lunch, afternoon, and evening, rounding off a day of excess with a nightcap or two. So, what to drink? With the winter holidays quickly approaching, it's time to update your drink list with festive cocktails! The 12 Drinks of Christmas are just as delicious while finishing up some holiday shopping online or watching a new holiday flick, as well.

Holidays are for celebrating! Getting together with family and friends is a time-honored tradition. It's time to start some new traditions with these special, unique drink recipes!

Each recipe was tested under strict conditions until taste perfection was achieved. Please enjoy responsibly~!

Having tried several, these are the most inventive, creative and refreshing, using local ingredients from the Baja. It's 5-o'clock somewhere! ~**Rusty & Jolene Beard, Goodyear, AZ. Professional grape and spirits testers**

'Handcrafted' cocktails made with love. Every drink is creative and thoughtfully constructed. Sitara uses local ingredients from her ranch in/and from Valle de Guadalupe. All locally sourced. Her cocktails are absolutely beautiful, delicious, creative and taste fabulous! No place like it in the Valle, truly unique experience. Don't miss out! ~**Morgan Launer, San Diego, CA. beer, wine, and spirits enthusiast**

A partridge in a pear tree
PEAR SPICED SANTA

A partridge in a pear tree
PEAR SPICED SANTA

Yes, absolutely shake up this fruity festive cocktail for Christmas breakfast! Permission granted.

Ingredients

Nob of fresh ginger
1 ½ oz LFA Unbarreled Brandy
¾ oz LFA Cinnamon Schnapps
¾ oz agave syrup
½ oz fresh lime juice
1 oz pear nectar
Dash of Angostura bitters
Ginger ale

Directions

Peel and coarsely chop the fresh ginger. Place in your cocktail shaker and vigorously muddle. Add the other ingredients with ice, minus the ginger ale and shake till chilled. Double strain into a rocks glass over a large cube of ice. Top with ginger ale. Garnish with a long cinnamon stick.

Two turtle doves
FROSTY TIRAMISU

Two turtle doves
FROSTY TIRAMISU

What could be more delectable than a boozy liquid tiramisu? This recipe is my personal riff on the popular That's Amore cocktail served at The Bar Room in New York. Pairs well with unwrapping Christmas gifts.

Ingredients

1 ½ oz LFA Triple Distilled Vodka
½ oz orange liqueur
¼ oz LFA F150 Fennel Liqueur
½ oz LFA Cinnamon Schnapps
¾ oz coffee liqueur
¼ oz honey
Lady fingers

Directions

Muddle 2-3 ladyfingers and reserve the crushed cookies in a small dish. Pour a little honey into a shallow dish and roll the outside of a cocktail glass in the syrup to act as an adhesive for the ground ladyfingers. Gently roll the outside of the glass in the ladyfinger crumbs to create a thick cookie rim. Wipe any crumbs out of the inside of the glass. Pour the remaining ingredients into your cocktail shaker, add ice and shake till chilled. Strain into your cookied-glass over a large ice cube.

NOTES

Three French hens ...
THYME INFUSED SALTY REINDEER

Three French hens …
THYME INFUSED SALTY REINDEER

Incidentally this refreshing cocktail pairs beautifully with Cornish game hens, a Christmas goose or your classic turkey supper.

Ingredients

Fresh thyme
2 oz LFA Triple Distilled Vodka
2 oz fresh grapefruit juice
½ oz fresh lime juice
½ oz simple syrup
1 Tbsp kosher salt

Directions

On a small plate pour approximately 1 tablespoon of kosher salt. Wet the rim of a chilled rocks glass with a quarter of a lime then dip or roll the wet edge of the glass into the salt. Snip several tablespoons of fresh thyme into your cocktail shaker and gently crush the leaves and stems to release the botanical oils and aromas. Add the rest of the ingredients with ice and shake till thoroughly chilled. Double strain into the salt rimmed glass over a large ice cube. Garnish with a sprig of fresh thyme.

Four calling birds …
'TIS THE SEASON SPRITZER

Four calling birds …
'TIS THE SEASON SPRITZER

Ingredients

1 ½ oz LFA Berry Brandy
½ oz orange liqueur
½ oz fresh lime juice
½ oz fresh lemon juice
¾ oz homemade grenadine syrup
Sparkling water

Directions

Pour all ingredients with ice, minus the sparkling water, into your cocktail shaker. Shake till well chilled. Strain into a coupe and top with sparkling water. Garnish with a lemon wheel.

Five golden rings …
GINGER GOLD FIZZ

Five golden rings …
GINGER GOLD FIZZ

I just can't get enough of Christmas spice and this lively sipper has just the right amount of ginger to keep your spirits fresh.

Ingredients

Nob of fresh ginger
1 ½ oz LFA Brandy
¾ oz fresh lemon juice
½ oz orange liqueur
½ oz sweet red vermouth
Splash of simple syrup
Splash of soda or sparkling wine

Directions

Peel and coarsely chop the ginger. Place it in your cocktail shaker and vigorously muddle. Add the rest of the ingredients minus the soda or sparkling wine with ice and shake till chilled. Fine strain into a chilled coupe. Garnish with an extra-long lemon twist.

Six geese a laying ...
MAPLE BRANDY SOUR

Six geese a laying …
MAPLE BRANDY SOUR

Sours are a traditional family of mixed drinks that include a base liquor, lemon or lime juice, a sweetener and egg white. You may omit the egg white if you choose but it adds a heavenly richness which elevates this cocktail without the extra calories of cream.

Ingredients

1 ½ oz LFA Unbarreled Brandy
¾ oz LFA Cinnamon Schnapps
½ oz LFA F150 Fennel Liqueur
¾ oz fresh lemon juice
¾ oz maple syrup
1 egg white

Directions

Carefully separate egg white from yolk and discard yolk. Pour egg white into you cocktail shaker with the other ingredients and vigorously dry shake (no ice). Be sure to have a firm grip on the lid of your shaker as the egg white will froth and expand creating pressure. Take the lid off, add ice and shake again till well chilled. Strain into a coupe and sprinkle with cinnamon.

Seven swans a swimming …
LIMONCELLO MERINGUE MARTINI

Seven swans a swimming …
LIMONCELLO MERINGUE MARTINI

Here I was looking for something truly extravagant to sip on. This gorgeous little number is balanced with the brightness of lemon juice and limoncello. The splash of vanilla ties it all together!

Ingredients

1 ½ oz LFA Triple Distilled Vodka
1 oz limoncello
½ oz fresh lemon juice
½ oz simple syrup
½ oz heavy cream
½ tsp pure vanilla extract
Optional egg white

If you want a truly frothy meringue, then start by carefully separating egg white from yolk and discard the yolk. Add all ingredients to cocktail shaker and dry shake vigorously to create maximum froth. Add ice and shake till chilled. Pour into a chilled martini glass. If you are omitting the egg white, simply add all other ingredients with ice to your shaker. Shake till well chilled and pour into your glass. Enjoy!

Eight maids a milking …
JINGLE BELL EGGNOG

Eight maids a milking …
JINGLE BELL EGGNOG

The creamy signature sipper of the holiday season, eggnog is the tasty descendent of Medieval posset, a super thick mix of hot milk, spirits and spices. It experienced a rebirth in American colonial times. George Washington even had an insanely strong recipe for this liquid custard that called for four different spirits: bourbon, rum, brandy and sherry! My tamer version only calls for two types of liquor: our fruity unbarreled Brandy and Cinnamon Schnapps. This should help get you through a long day of festive family time.

Ingredients

1 oz LFA Cinnamon Schnapps
½ oz LFA Unbarreled Brandy
Bar spoon simple syrup
1 ½ oz full fat eggnog, plus extra for garnishing
Spiced cookies, crushed
Cinnamon sugar
Freshly ground nutmeg

Directions

Wet the rim of a chilled glass with the extra eggnog and dip into the crushed spiced cookies. Mix the cinnamon schnapps, brandy, simple syrup, and full fat eggnog in a cocktail shaker with ice. Strain and pour the mixture into the rimmed glass. Garnish with a sprinkle of cinnamon sugar and freshly ground nutmeg and serve.

NOTES

Nine ladies dancing …
GINGERBREAD MARTINI

When pumpkin spice season ends it's time for gingerbread! Sweet, spicy, and comforting, gingerbread is the epitome of holiday cheer. Fresh ginger and molasses come together in a homemade gingerbread syrup to elevate this cocktail to winter holiday delights. Consider this one Santa's Little Helper.

Ingredients

1 oz LFA Triple Distilled Vodka
1 oz LFA Cinnamon Schnapps
¾ oz amaretto
½ oz homemade gingerbread syrup plus 2 Tbsp, divided
¼ cup crushed gingerbread cookies

Directions

Pour 2 tablespoons of homemade gingerbread syrup onto a small plate. On an additional small plate pour the ¼ cup of crushed gingerbread cookies. Rim your chilled martini glass in the gingerbread syrup and then in the crushed cookies. Set aside. Add the rest of the ingredients to your cocktail shaker with ice. Shake vigorously till well chilled. Strain into cookie rimmed martini glass.

Ten lords a leaping …
GINGERBREAD LATTE

Ten lords a leaping …
GINGERBREAD LATTE

This warming drink is all the best parts of an iced gingerbread cake mixed with hot coffee, a splash of Baileys, homemade gingerbread syrup and topped with whipped cream. It's winter wonderland in a mug!

Ingredients

1 oz LFA Unbarreled Brandy
3 oz coffee
½ oz homemade gingerbread syrup
½ oz Baileys
Whipped cream
Directions

In a glass mug, add the Brandy and gingerbread syrup. Stir to combine. Pour the coffee into the mug and top with Baileys Irish Cream. Stir gently. Top with whipped cream. Sip merrily.

Eleven pipers piping …
POINSETTIA PUNCH

Eleven pipers piping …
POINSETTIA PUNCH

I'm pretty sure if Santa was offered a cocktail menu instead of a glass of milk he'd choose this tasty and festive Poinsettia Punch. But since we don't promote drinking and sleigh-flying it's probably best to just shake one up for yourself!

Ingredients

1 ½ oz LFA Berry Brandy
¾ oz LFA Cinnamon Schnapps
½ oz maraschino cherry liqueur
½ oz fresh lemon juice
Bar spoon homemade grenadine syrup
simple syrup
Cinnamon sugar for rim
For a less boozy alternative, add 1 oz cranberry juice

Directions

On a small plate pour approximately 1 tablespoon of simple syrup. On an additional small plate pour approximately 1 tablespoon of cinnamon sugar. Dip the rim of a large rocks glass into the simple syrup, then dip in the cinnamon sugar. In your cocktail shaker add the rest of the ingredients with ice and shake vigorously till chilled. Strain into your rimmed rocks glass over a large cube of ice. Garnish with whole cranberries on a cocktail spear.

NOTES

Twelve drummers drumming …

HOT BUTTERED BRANDY

Twelve drummers drumming …
HOT BUTTERED BRANDY

Someone can just say "hot buttered rum" and you can feel your mouth salivate. This notion of mixing up hot water, liquor, spices, and butter goes back to our colonial roots when the rum flowed more than the whiskey. In my riff we use a combination of LFA Unbarreled Brandy and Cinnamon Schnapps to make a tasty, luscious treat.

Ingredients

1 cup water
¼ stick unsalted butter
1/8 cup packed dark brown sugar
½ tsp cinnamon
¼ tsp freshly grated nutmeg
1/8 tsp ground cloves
Pinch salt
¼ cup LFA Unbarreled Brandy
¼ cup LFA Cinnamon Schnapps

Directions

Bring water, butter, brown sugar, cinnamon, nutmeg, cloves, and salt to a boil in a 1 ½ - to 2-quart saucepan over moderately high heat. Reduce heat and simmer, whisking occasionally,

10 minutes. Remove from heat and stir in brandy and Cinnamon Schnapps. Serve hot.

NOTES

Bonus Cocktail
BLUE CHRISTMAS

Bonus Cocktail
BLUE CHRISTMAS

If you're looking for a unique holiday drink with a stunning presentation, try my Blue Christmas cocktail! You'll be anything but blue after one sip of this bright and lively cocktail.

Ingredients

½ oz blue curacao
¾ oz LFA Triple Distilled Vodka
¾ oz LFA Unbarreled Brandy
1 barspoon maraschino cherry liqueur
1 barspoon (½ oz) simple syrup
½ oz fresh lemon juice
1 Tbsp sugar for rimming glass
Lemon wedges for rimming and garnish

Directions

Pour sugar onto a small plate. Rim a chilled martini glass using a lemon wedge and dip into sugar. In a shaker filled with ice, combine the liquors, simple syrup, and lemon juice. Shake to chill. Place one large ice cube in your rimmed martini glass. Strain the drink into glass. Garnish with lemon curls or wedges.

NOTES

A WORD ON ICE

Size matters. When creating a craft cocktail, every detail counts. Even the size and shape of the ice that's used can have a huge impact on your finished drink. Small surface ice cubes and pebble ice melt faster, diluting a drink, which may be desirable in some cocktails but discouraged in others. I like to use pebble ice in my cocktail shaker not only because it chills the drink ingredients quickly but because it adds just that little bit of water that can balance out a boozy beverage. In the glass however I prefer large cubes or spheres which melt slowly, keeping the cocktail chilled without over diluting it. The visual impact is great too and presentation, especially when you're serving friends and family over the holidays, is part of the pleasure. The quality of the water matters too! If you wouldn't dream of drinking your tap water, then don't make your ice with it. I always use filtered spring water.

A WORD ON GARNISHES

Garnishes add visual appeal, subtle aromas and flavors to our drinks. And though it may seem like a minor, unimportant component, the presentation of a well-mixed cocktail enhances the drinking experience. The garnish is the final touch, meant to complement, accentuate, and elevate all of the elements of the finished cocktail. Like picking out a scarf or a pair of earrings to set off an outfit, so too, does the garnish help communicate the personality of the drink, filling out the cocktail experience.

Our memories and emotions are wrapped up in our senses. So. the look, temperature, aromas, and flavors of a good cocktail are a complete experience. Therefore, a beautifully crafted drink can enhance any festive occasion and become memorable in its own right. And isn't that what we're doing when we get together with friends and family over the holidays? Making memories.

Garnishes can be simple or fancy, edible or inedible, large, or small, a part of the drink or meant to be discarded. There are many types of garnishes: salt, sugar or crushed cookie rims, twists, fruit, botanicals, flowers, spices, bitters, food, objects … Have fun with your garnishes and let your imagination go wild.

A WORD ON BAR TOOLS

It's not necessary to have a bunch of fancy tools or an elaborate set up to make a good cocktail. That said, a few tools are extremely helpful. I love my cocktail shaker with its built-in strainer but if you don't have one you can improvise. A Boston shaker, for example is simply a two-piece shaker consisting of a glass and a metal tin. A common combination is a 16 oz. glass with a 28 oz. metal tin. Some bartenders prefer using two metal tins. But if you don't have either of these handy, a mason jar with a lid will work in a pinch! You'll want to have a small strainer or sieve nearby to strain out small ice shards that would otherwise dilute your drink, as well as muddled fruit, herbs, or aromatics.

I've learned that balance and precision are essential to crafting a delicious and delectable cocktail. So, I highly recommend that you put jiggers at the top of your list for indispensable bar tools. Some bartenders prefer free pouring which is a fast and easy method for standard well drinks but can easily get out of control when mixing a craft cocktail with multiple ingredients. I take pride in creating perfectly balanced drinks and if you follow my recipes and measure correctly. I think you will enjoy the results.

I like to muddle fresh ginger and other aromatics in my holiday drinks. So, a muddler is a handy tool to have around. What is a muddler? Simply a blunt tool used to smash and mix cocktail ingredients to extract oils, juices, and aromas. A muddler can be made of polished wood, metal, granite or any hard, food grade material.

Other essential tools would be a citrus reamer for making fresh juices, a sharp paring knife, a sharp peeler, a zester, and a pair of scissors for snipping herbs and flowers.

Less essential but really great if as a home bartender you are really getting into the game: bar mats to catch spillage, long handled bar spoons (They hold 5 milliliters or one teaspoon of liquid), and a bar spoon with a hole for scooping out cocktail cherries or olives without their liquid. If you like straws in your drinks, consider washable and reusable straws like stainless steel or silicone. And for your fun and fancy garnishes consider environmentally friendly drink spears made of bamboo or washable and reusable stainless steel. The planet thanks you!

ABOUT US

Sitara Monica Perez is a winemaker and Todd Michael Truelson is a distiller, both live and work in beautiful Valle de Guadalupe, Baja California, Mexico. Both Sitara and Todd have had many careers but have discovered a new vocation working together to create unique and delicious artisanal spirits. Todd built a "private cocktail club" at the winery site which they've named La Flama Azúl (the blue flame). Sitara subsequently discovered a new passion in mixology. You can find Todd and Sitara at their ranch, El Corcho Rosa (the pink cork) in Valle de Guadalupe, Baja, California, Mexico, where you can sample and purchase Sitara's Valle Girl Vino wines, delicious food, as well as La Flama Azúl spirits and craft cocktails. Come join us~!

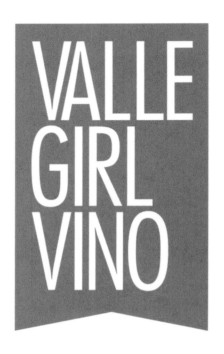

Valle Girl Vino at El Corcho Rosa
Instagram: @vallegirlvino
https://www.vallegirlvino.com

CONTACT US
sitara.perez@gmail.com
+52 646 198 4024

Made in the USA
Middletown, DE
16 December 2021